Super Senses

Raintree

www.raintreepublishers.co.uk

Visit our website to find out more information about **Raintree** books.

To order:

 Phone 44 (0) 1865 888112

Send a fax to 44 (0) 1865 314091

Visit the Raintree Bookshop at **www.raintreepublishers.co.uk** to browse our catalogue and order online.

First published in Great Britain by Raintree,
Halley Court, Jordan Hill, Oxford OX2 8EJ,
part of Harcourt Education.
Raintree is a registered trademark of Harcourt
Education Ltd.

Editorial: Kate Bellamy
Design: Jo Hinton-Malivoire and bigtop
Illustrations: Darren Lingard
Picture Research: Hannah Taylor and Fiona Orbell
Production: Helen McCreath

Originated by Chroma Graphics (Overseas) Pte. Ltd
Printed and bound in China by
South China Printing Company

ISBN 1 406 20023 9 (hardback)
ISBN 978 1 406 20023 2 (hardback)
10 09 08 07 06
10 9 8 7 6 5 4 3 2 1
ISBN 1 406 20030 1 (paperback)
ISBN 978 1 406 20030 0 (paperback)
11 10 09 08 07
10 9 8 7 6 5 4 3 2 1

British Library Cataloguing in Publication Data
Mackill, Mary
Touching – (Super Senses)
612.8'8
A full catalogue record for this book is available
from the British Library.

Acknowledgements
The publishers would like to thank the following
for permission to reproduce photographs:
Alamy Images pp. **4** (Andre Jenny), **9**
(RubberBall), **5**, **23b** (STOCK IMAGEPIXLAND),
11, **23e** (Thinkstock); Corbis pp. **13**, **21a**, **22**
(royalty free), **16** (Michael Keller); FLPA p. **19**;
Getty Images pp. **12** (Altrendo), **10** (Digital
Vision), **14** (National Geographic), **6**, **15a**, **15b**,
15c, **21b**, **21c**, **21d**, **23a**, **23d** (Photodisc), **17**,
(Stone), **7**, **18** (Taxi); Harcourt Education Ltd
p. **20** (Tudor Photography); Photodisc p. **15d**.

Cover photograph reproduced with permission of
Getty Images/The Image Bank.

Every effort has been made to contact copyright
holders of any material reproduced in this book.
Any omissions will be rectified in subsequent
printings if notice is given to the publishers.

The paper used to print this book comes from
sustainable resources.

Disclaimer
All the Internet addresses (URLs) given in this
book were valid at the time of going to press.
However, due to the dynamic nature of the
Internet, some addresses may have changed, or
sites may have changed or ceased to exist since
publication. While the author and publishers
regret any inconvenience this may cause readers,
no responsibility for any such changes can be
accepted by either the author or the publishers.

Contents

Some words are shown in bold, **like this**. They are explained in the glossary on page 23.

What are *my* senses?

You have five **senses**. They help you to see, hear, taste, smell, and touch things.

Pretend you are at the beach.

What can you touch?

Touching is one of your five senses.

What do I use to touch?

Your **skin** can **sense** touch.

You have skin all over your body.

This girl can feel the water splashing on her skin!

How does *my* sense of touch work?

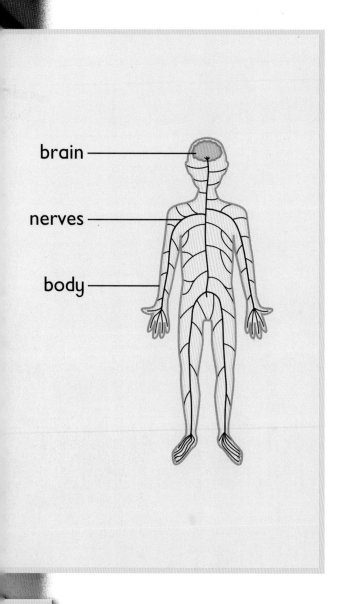

brain

nerves

body

Your **skin** has lots of **nerves**.

When you touch something, the nerves send a message to your brain.

Your brain picks up the message.

Your brain would tell you that the cat feels soft.

What can I touch?

Your **skin** can feel soft things, like this pillow.

A slide is hard
and **smooth**.

Would you like to
go down a slide
that is **rough**?

How does touching help me?

Your **sense** of touch helps you to stay safe.

It stops you touching hot things that will hurt you.

It feels good when someone you love hugs you.

How can I help my sense of touch?

Some things are dangerous to touch.

Look at things before you touch them.

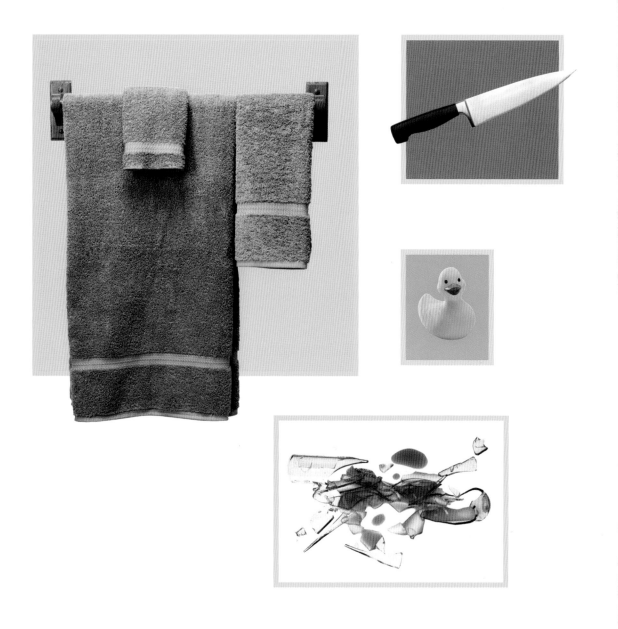

Which of these are safe to touch?

How can I look after my sense of touch?

It is easy to hurt your **skin**.

Watch out for hot or sharp things!

Wear shoes when you play outside.

Shoes stop you hurting the skin on your feet.

Animals can touch too!

Some animals touch things to find out where they are.

feelers

This mole uses feelers on its nose to touch.

It helps the mole to find food to eat.

Test your sense of touch

Cover your eyes.

Touch different fruit with your hands.

Is the fruit soft or hard, **rough** or **smooth**?

	hard	soft
rough	 pineapple	kiwi
smooth	apple	pear

Touching is super!

Your **sense** of touch:

- helps you to work out what something is

- tells you what is safe to touch

- means you can hug the people you love!

Glossary

 **nerves** parts inside your body. Nerves work with the brain to sense things.

 rough something that is rough feels bumpy

 **sense** something that helps you to see, touch, taste, smell, and hear the things around you

 **skin** the outside covering of your body

 **smooth** something that is smooth feels even

Index

Note to Parents and Teachers

Reading for information is an important part of a child's literacy development. Learning begins with a question about something. Help children think of themselves as investigators and researchers by encouraging their questions about the world around them. Each chapter in this book begins with a question. Read the question together. Look at the pictures. Talk about what you think the answer might be. Then read the text to find out if your predictions were correct. Think of other questions you could ask about the topic, and discuss where you might find the answers. Assist children in using the picture glossary and the index to practice new vocabulary and research skills.